What Acts Were Intolerable Acts?

US History Textbook

Children's American History

Speedy Publishing LLC

40 E. Main St. #1156

Newark, DE 19711

www.speedypublishing.com

Copyright 2017

In this book we will learn about the Intolerable Acts, which were laws the British Parliament passed to try and control the people in the American Colonies. These Acts led to the start of the revolution and America seeking freedom from British rule. Read on to find out why!

These acts were passed by the British as punishment for their acts during the Boston Tea Party and were sometimes called the Punitive Acts.

While the British felt these acts would help to keep control in America, they resulted in an opposite effect and caused several people to join the rebels.

Read further to learn about these five "intolerable" laws.

The British Parliament became fed up with the antics of the colonists. They could handle letters or boycotts. They could handle rebellious legislature and would hassle customs officials.

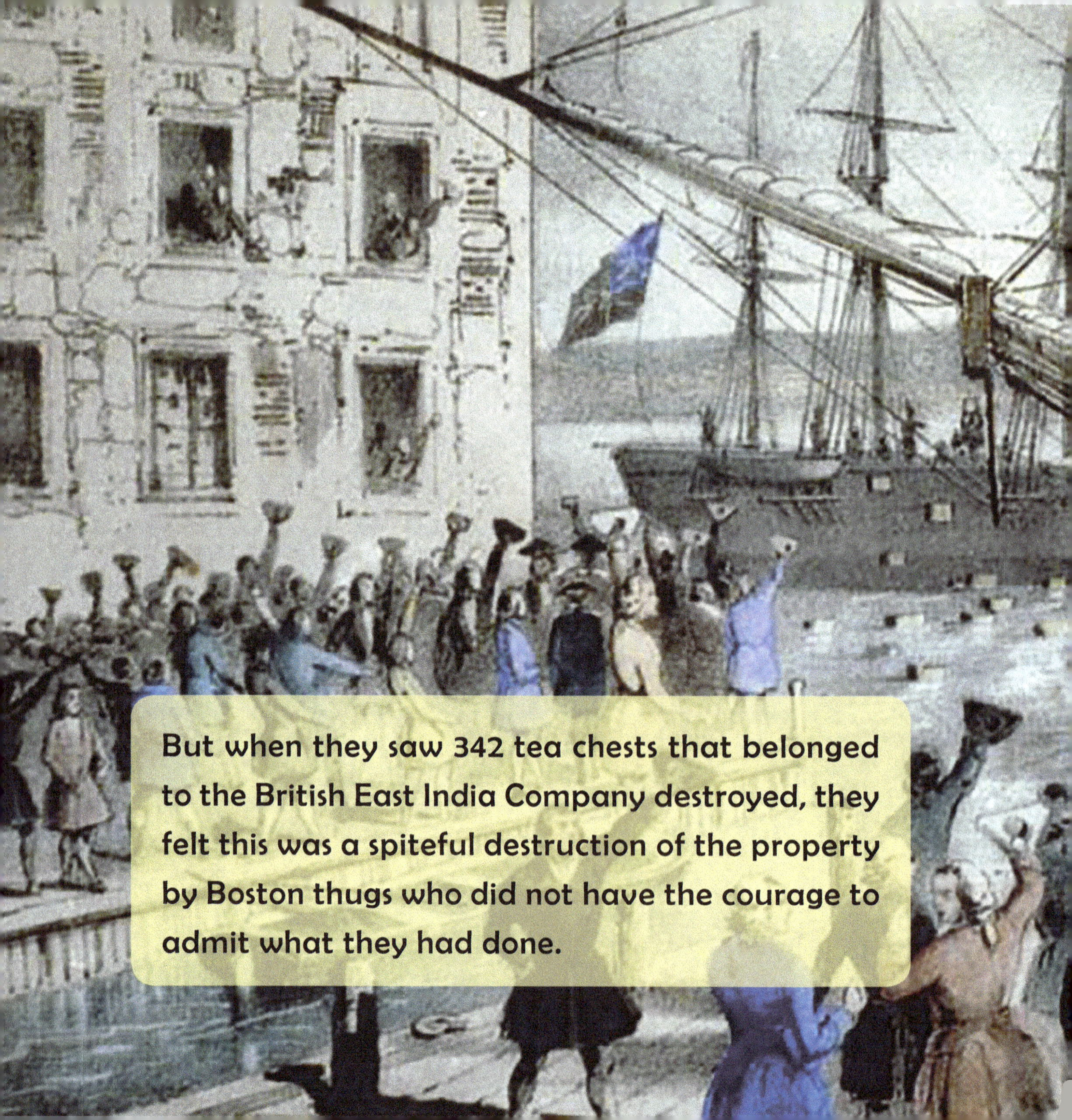

But when they saw 342 tea chests that belonged to the British East India Company destroyed, they felt this was a spiteful destruction of the property by Boston thugs who did not have the courage to admit what they had done.

The Intolerable Acts and the Boston Tea Party
Tensions were high which led to these two incidents which then led to creation of the Intolerable Acts.

The Boston Massacre, occurring on March 5, 1770, when the British soldiers, who lived in the city, fired into a mob killing 5 American civilians

The Boston Tea Party occurring on December 16, 1773 was in protest by Boston Colonists against the Tea Tax. The Sons of Liberty, dressed like Mohawk Indians, let the Boston patriots, and proceeded to raid three British ships in the Boston harbor, and then dumped 342 boxes of tea in the water.

Most of the British people, along with King George III, and the British government which was led by Lord North were angered when they discovered the Boston colonists had thrown their tea into the salt water.

The British Parliament then proceeded to pass the Intolerable Acts as an act of punishment.

They decided someone had to pay.

The British referred to these measures as the Coercive Acts. The harbor was closed for trade until compensation was made to the tea owners.

The only items allowed in the port were firewood and food. They banned town meets, and increased authority to the royal governor.

The British Commander of the North American forces, General Gage, was then named as Massachusetts' governor. This meant that the British officials and troops would be tried for murder outside of Massachusetts.

The British officers had greater freedom when they offered to provide private housing for their soldiers.

The relationship between British Parliament and the Thirteen Colonies had slowly worsened when the Seven Years' War ended in 1763.

This had put the British government into deep debt, and the Parliament set forth measures increasing tax revenue to be received from these colonies.

Parliament then believed that acts including the Stamp Act and the Townshend Acts were a valid way to have the colonies pay the costs of keeping the Empire.

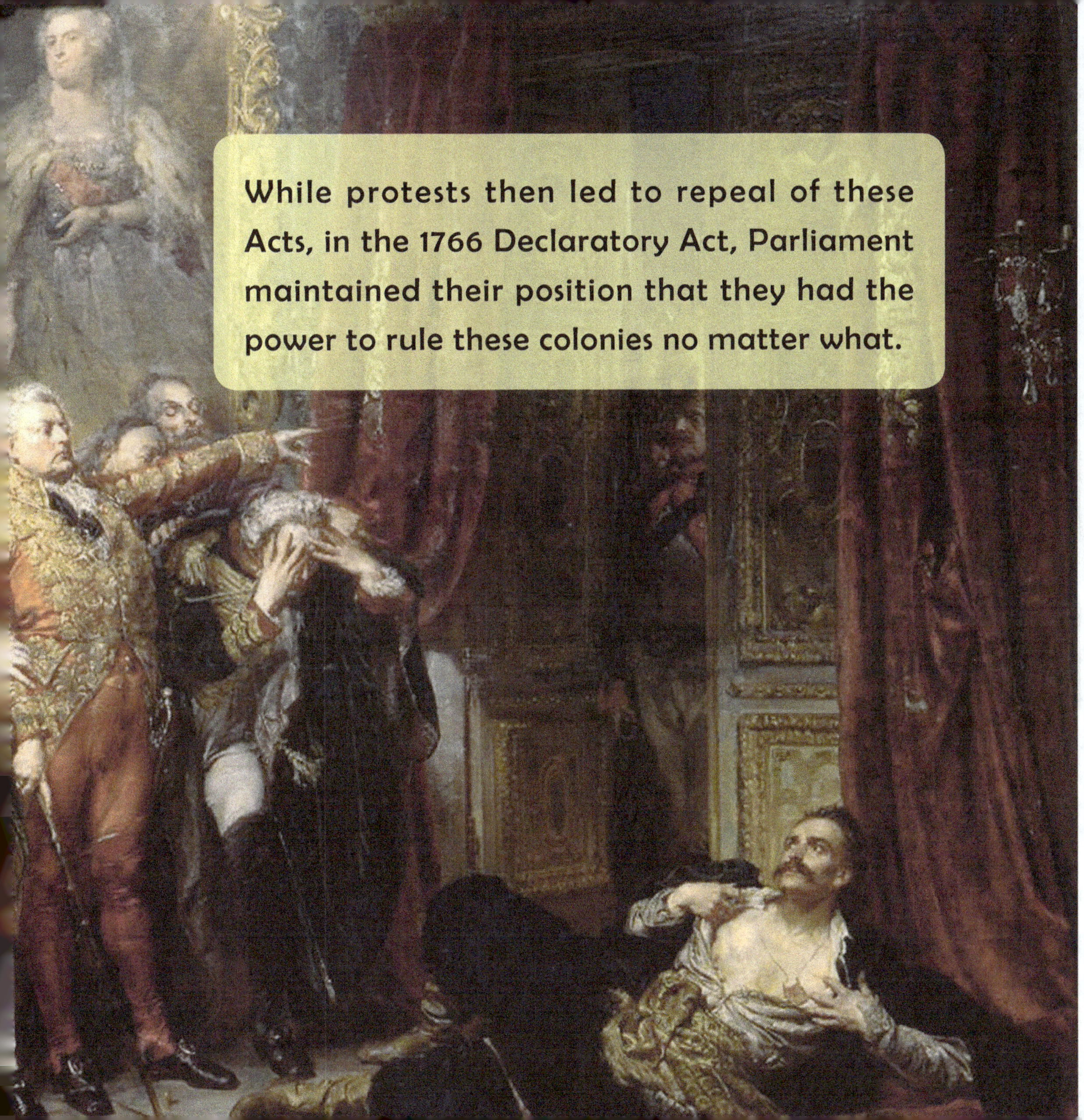

While protests then led to repeal of these Acts, in the 1766 Declaratory Act, Parliament maintained their position that they had the power to rule these colonies no matter what.

The Massachusetts Government Act and the Quartering Act provided Massachusetts' governor with control of this colony, instead of its people having control. Attempting to intimidate Boston's residents, General Thomas Gage was appointed by King George III, as Massachusetts' military governor in May of 1774.

After the Boston Massacre, he was quoted to say "America is a mere bully, from one end to the other, and the Bostonians by far are the greatest bullies". It was now clear that martial law was imposed and civil law was suspended.

The Five Acts

Boston Port Act

This became the first Intolerable Act to pass. It was in direct punishment to Boston for its Boston Tea Party.

The act closed Boston's port to all ships until the tea they had dumped in the harbor was paid for.

They thought it was unfair since it punished all Boston's citizens instead only the few that were involved in the dumping of the tea. Several other American colonies sent Boston supplies.

This act changed Massachusetts' government. More power was given to the governor, appointed by Great Britain, and took power away from the colonists. Many government officials that had formerly been elected by the people were not appointed by their governor.

The act also said that only one town meeting could take place each year. The entire Massachusetts colony was angered by this act and it instilled fear into other colonies. The other colonies felt that they would be next.

Administration of Justice Act

This act gave the governor power to move trials against the government officials to Great Britain. They felt that this gave the government officials too much protection. Trial witnesses would need to go to Britain in order to testify against an official.

This made it nearly impossible to get a conviction. Some of the colonists referred to this as the "Murder Act" as they felt it allowed them to get away with murder.

Quartering Act of 1774

This act was an expansion of the Quartering Act of 1765. It ruled that the colonies had to offer barracks for the British soldiers. If no barracks were available, they could be provided with housing in homes, barns, and hotels.

Quebec Act

This act extended the British Canadian land south to the Ohio Valley. It also ruled that the Quebec Province be a Catholic province. While this act was not in direct response to the Boston Tea Party, it passed the same time as the other acts.

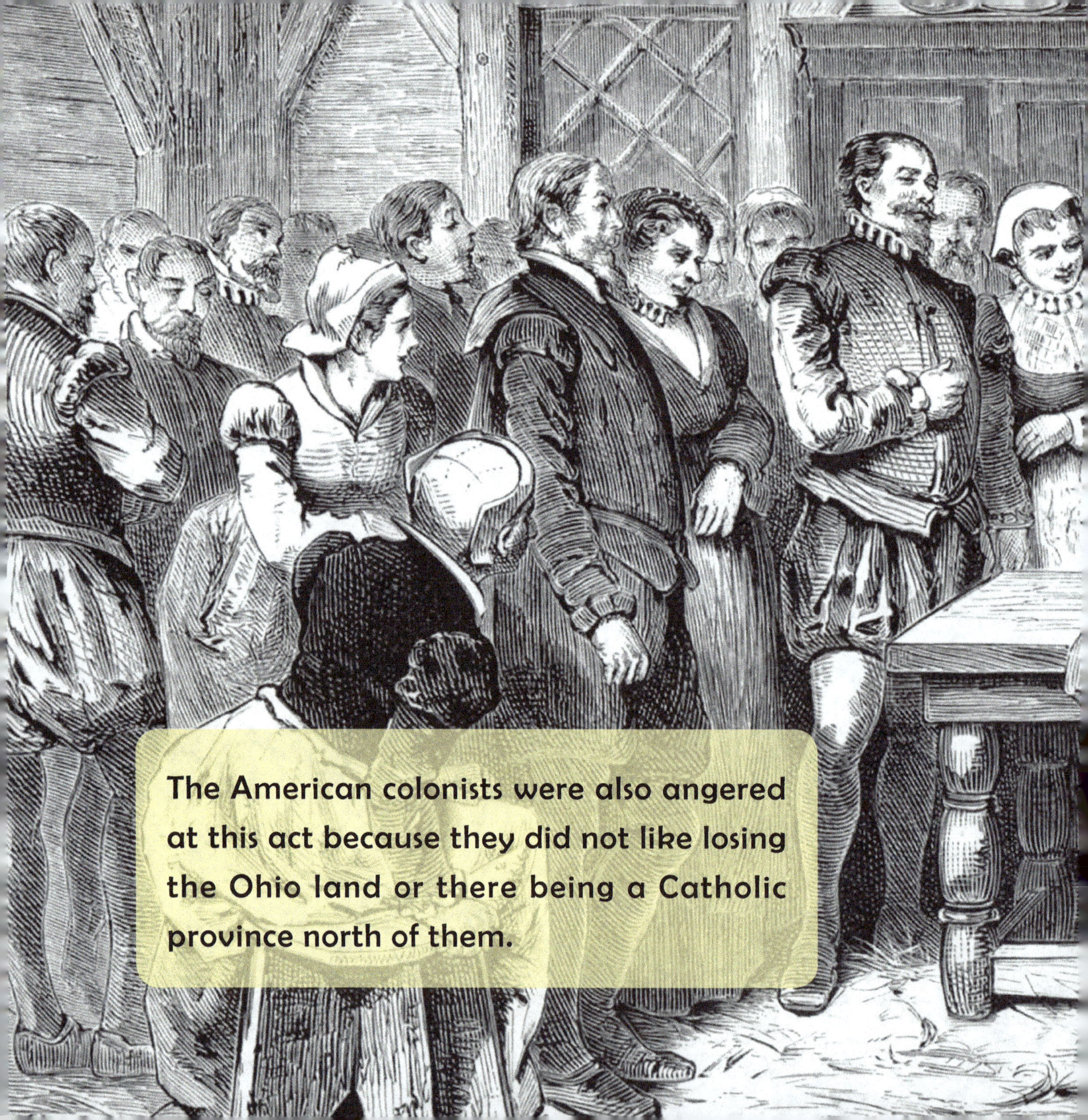

The American colonists were also angered at this act because they did not like losing the Ohio land or there being a Catholic province north of them.

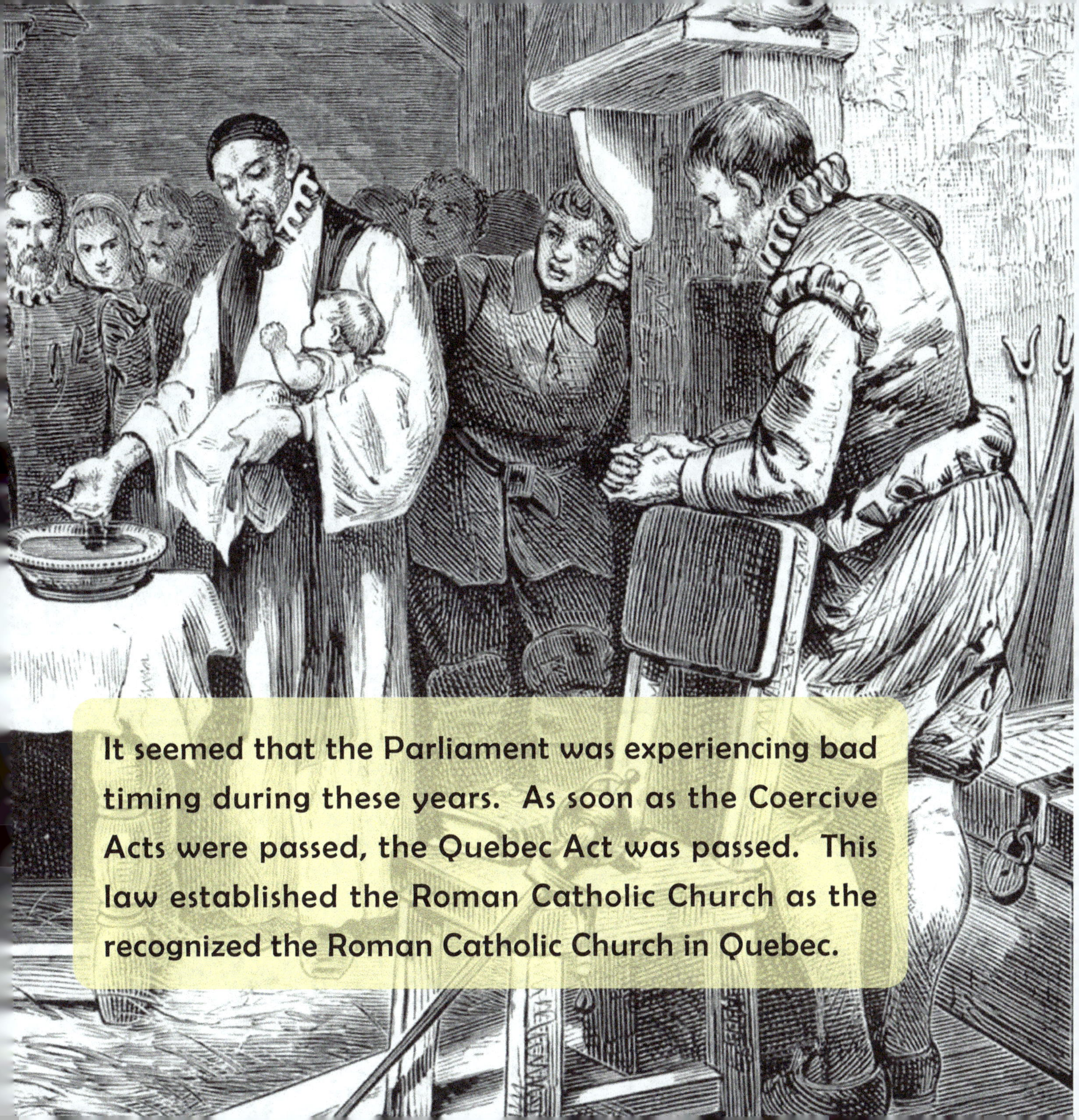

It seemed that the Parliament was experiencing bad timing during these years. As soon as the Coercive Acts were passed, the Quebec Act was passed. This law established the Roman Catholic Church as the recognized the Roman Catholic Church in Quebec.

Rather than the elected body, a council which was appointed would then make decisions for the colony. Quebec's boundaries were then extended to Ohio.

In light of passage of this Act, anger spread throughout all 13 colonies. The British Crown then granted land in Quebec to the French that the Americans wanted.

The broadening of tolerance to the Catholics was seen as a hostile act by Americans which were mostly predominant.

Another blow shook this democracy with establishment of the direct rule in Quebec. While the British did not connect the Quebec Act and the Coercive Act, they were seen by the Americans as malicious deeds and became known as the Intolerable Act.

The Intolerable Acts turned out to be a uniting cry for the American patriots. They believed the acts did away with several of their basic freedoms. These acts, in several ways, help unify the Colonies and directed them closer to the revolution.

It became clear throughout the colonies that what happened in Massachusetts might occur anywhere. The beleaguered colonies received supplies from the other colonies.

An intercolonial conference was then called, the first since the Stamp Act Crisis. Under these dire events, the First Continental Congress assembled on September 5, 1774, in Philadelphia.

The Declaration of Rights was issued by
the Continental Congress in response to
the Intolerable Acts. This declaration set
forth the colonial objections to the Acts
and listed the colonial grievances.

This was like the Declaration of Rights and Grievances of 1765, which was passed through the Stamp Act which had occurred ten years previously.

A boycott of British trade was put in placeuntil the grievances were settled and the Intolerable Acts had been revoked.

Great Britain had hoped that the Coercive Acts would isolate the Massachusetts radicals and lead American colonists to concede to the authority of British Parliament over their elected legislatures. However, this risk backfired and made it difficult for the colony moderates to speak in their favor.

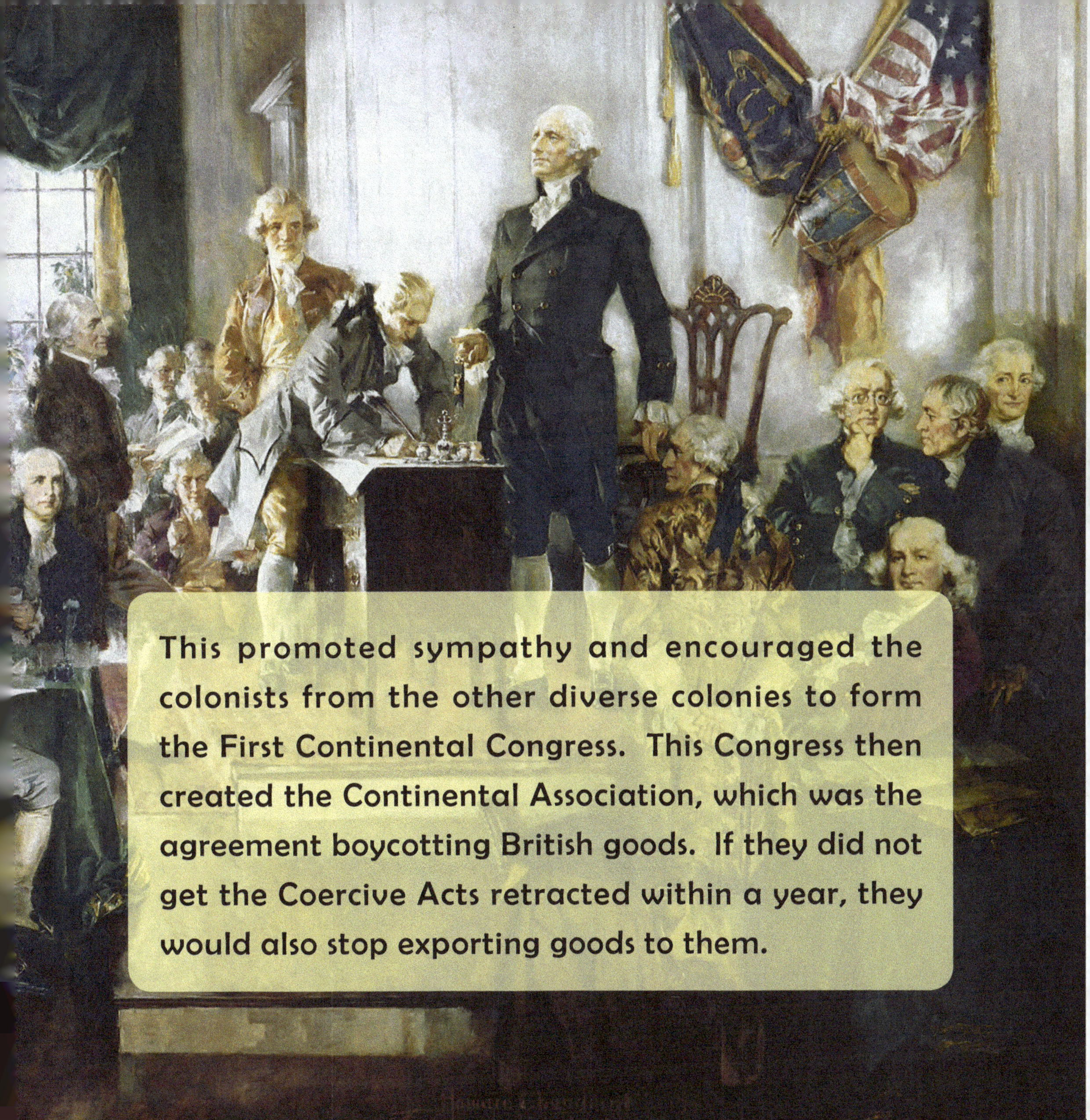

This promoted sympathy and encouraged the colonists from the other diverse colonies to form the First Continental Congress. This Congress then created the Continental Association, which was the agreement boycotting British goods. If they did not get the Coercive Acts retracted within a year, they would also stop exporting goods to them.

This Congress also agreed to support Massachusetts in case they were attacked, meaning that all colonies would be involved in the American Revolutionary War at Lexington and Concord.

In April of 1775, the American Revolutionary War began as tensions got worse, which led to the signing of the declaration of an independent United States of America in 1776, which we know as the Declaration of Independence which is celebrated on July 4 ever year.

To learn about the Intolerable Acts, the Continental Congress, the Boston Tea Party, and other historical events be sure to research the internet, go to your local library, and ask questions of your teachers, family, and friends.

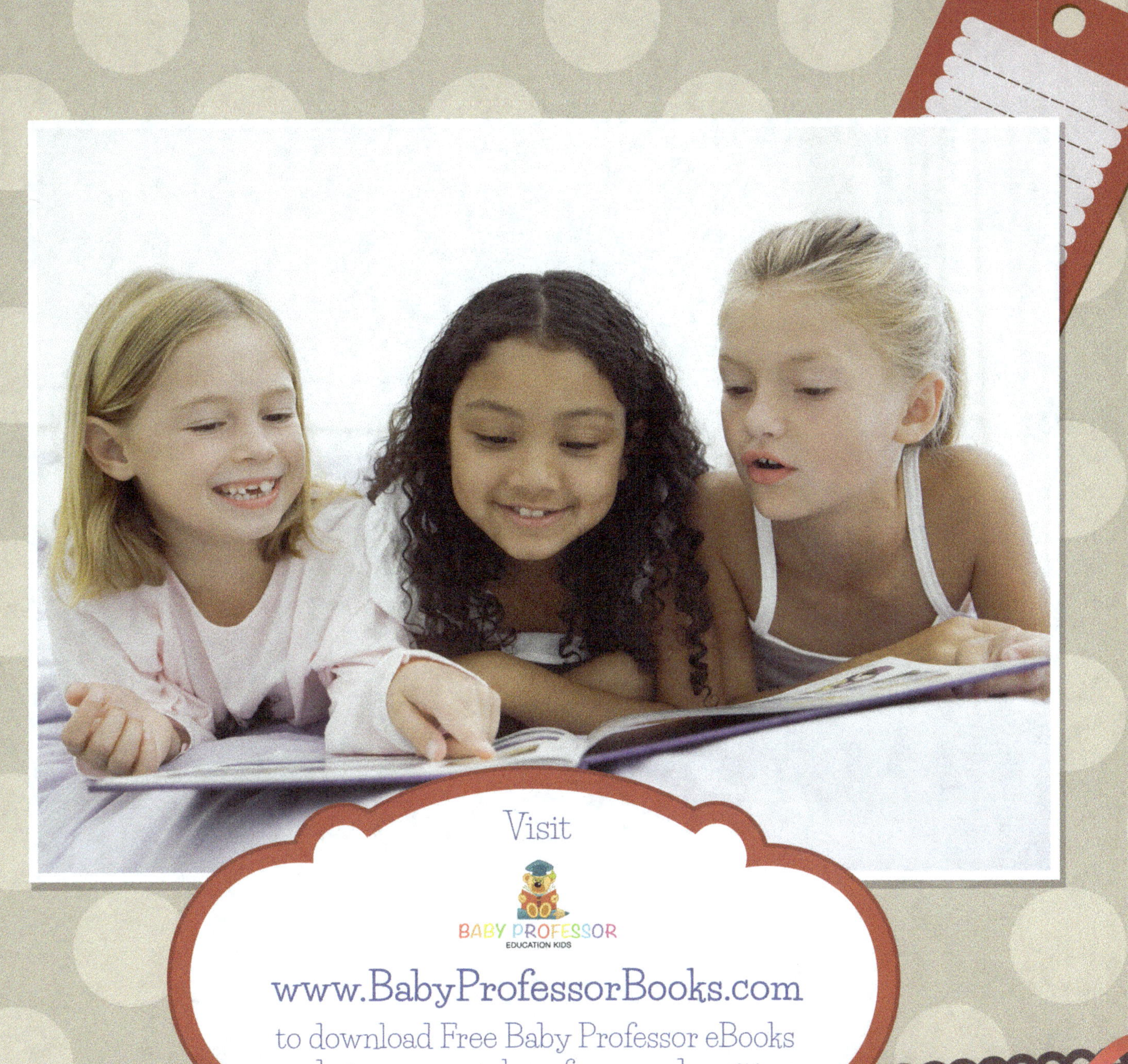
Visit
BABY PROFESSOR
EDUCATION KIDS
www.BabyProfessorBooks.com
to download Free Baby Professor eBooks
and view our catalog of new and exciting
Children's Books